Forty Acres and a Mule
(Poetry)

Fonkeng E.f

Langaa Research & Publishing CIG
Mankon, Bamenda

Publisher:
Langaa RPCIG
Langaa Research & Publishing Common Initiative Group
P.O. Box 902 Mankon
Bamenda
North West Region
Cameroon
Langaagrp@gmail.com
www.langaa-rpcig.net

Distributed in and outside N. America by African Books Collective
orders@africanbookscollective.com
www.africanbookcollective.com

ISBN: 9956-790-63-X

DISCLAIMER
All views expressed in this publication are those of the author and do not necessarily reflect the views of Langaa RPCIG.

Dedication

Rex Nettleford+, Francis Bebey+, Francis
Wache
Mentors far and near, past, present
The nursery, even to them, unbeknown
On which this seed has grown

Enambah, Ebamu, Elale, Forsack, Eba'ah
All who seek not to survive but to live

Table of Contents

Author's Note

These traveler's expressions of impressions collected across cultural and psychological spaces portray the two sides of this coin called life, oftentimes belligerent toward each other. Like the dishonoured promise made to each freed African of America at Emancipation (of forty acres and a mule), these lines, put together, cast light on the dream of total freedom and the daunting contradictions inherent in its being and attainment. They represent a dialectic, the spoke in the wheels of our bicycle, as we engage in this seemingly unending journey toward the shadow only of the *good life*, ceaselessly jettisoning virtue against vice.

At a level, they confront a certain tyranny of thought, in more ways than one, challenging us to go beyond the comfort of our thought and socialization and to dare to look at the world through prisms hitherto only dreamed of. For example, *Downside Up,* in an unassuming manner, turns the mundane perception of blackness on its head, revealing a refreshing (and positive) conception of that state of being.

At yet another level, this challenge is portrayed in relation to not only language but also to the cannons of poetry (with *sextroversy* and *sextination* representing examples of the former). A too tight a reliance on 'traditional' verse and rhyme, for example, engenders the risk of blurring the message beyond any significance. Because literary writing in this so-called global society may rightfully be considered as war by other means, the reader will quickly observe the, literally, take-no-prisoner approach embedded in many of these pieces – the generalized despondency on the ground and the unprecedented cacophony of voices in the 'global village' calling for nothing less.

The general conclusion of this collection would, therefore, be the deferment of the promise of living even as these poems constitute a harkening for us to live beyond existence.

Fonkeng E.f
Odawa, November, 2012

The Promise

Epasa Moto

Half human, half deity
Today as yesterday
Matters not whoever saw Him
The legend is sacred

Come another hunting season
Fako's trails open for the long trek
In search of every blessing
They embark, each with an offering

With afflictions, to Him,
Of every persuasion, they come
The God-man will bless – and pity
Of Epasa Moto, their faith is stoic

The centre of their being
Part human, part deity
In his abode, somewhere
Up the mountain of fire

Notes:
Epasa Moto – according to a legend of the Mokwe [ethnic group inhabiting the mountain's lower slopes], part-human, part-deity that lives up the Fako
Fako (also called Mount Cameroon) – highest peak in West/Central Africa. Found in Buea, Cameroon.

Epitaph (The Torch)

The African
Stoic defender
of the Cause, Africa
He dreamed,
believed
thought
lived
taught,
No home had he
Because he believed
in the African home
Utopian, they mocked
Nubian, he answered
Just the Torch you need
Out of this long, haunted Dark Night

Solidarity

Take on them, big time
Still, they soldier on
Like a mustard seed
Will not die, this breed
Before society's cold suit
Against their hot pursuit

A silent meet
Between strangers
The transformation
An instant friendship
The bridge,
A cigarette and its after glow

What light for a global village estranged?

The Heart

That heart is a bird
Flies oblivious to frontiers,
Human and geographical
Rests where it will

Like a leaf
Goes with the wind
Straddles the compounds
Of even enemy-neighbours

Like my palm
Must cringe
To a rough handshake
But will accept it warm

This heart is green,
Animal, and human
The egg I carry with care

Nature's Honeymoon

I put on my sunscreen
Picked up the ice-cream
Biked to the park
My sack on my back
I met my friend Mark
We sat in the park
Each on a mat
Eating each our snack
'Till it was dark

Hail, this songbird
Time to sleep, sit, sing
Where we would rather run
Into today's rain

Time to stand, stare, smell the roses
Put for another day
What we won't do today
Hail, the breaks of this motor

Nature's Honeymoon – Sequel

Let the world pass by
And the helter-skelter bandwagon
The brother's lament, too
Mi cann sleep, me by-pass

Happy for they who invented nothing
The echo in a brother's line
Nothing they have to lose
This journeyman will go – with the stars

Won't be crushed in the rush
The rat-race to finish fast and first
Will stop to smell the roses
Arrive alive, in one piece – with the stars

Won't dance to the music
The helter-skelter bandit band
This journeyman will dance – to be alive
With the rain, sun – or the stars

Will dare to sleep, sit, sing a song
Stand, stare, smile at sunset
Pen a poem, maybe two – for serenity
Time, there is, in this life, alas

Note:
Mi cann sleep – Caribbean Creole for *I can't buy sleep*!

Come and See (America Wonder)

One eye, ear, arm or leg
No blemish if American
Will snug with the pig
If a Yankee middle name

Swim, fly, run, walk, crawl to
Sweep America, no problem
When I see America Wonder
That, my Dream Apple

The barks from my backyard
Their curative juices will tap
Clean, cook, bathe with and ingest
If from America Wonder

Peaks of abuses, bruises, defeats
The malefactor of a mind
Still no divorce will this mind seek
From its Soul – America Wonder!

Nothing
(Tribute to Lumumba-Malcom X)

It's nothing
Only a wolf in sheep's skin
The posturing saint
Dumb to his boys in the hood
Passes them for a misguided few

Have nothing
With the four season chameleon
A poisoned weed
Growing tall above the crops
Its thorns wind-dance in full view

It's nothing
A handshake
With a book called holy
Wrapped in thorns and bombs
Your blood's spilled and sucked, no hue

Say nothing
You're no beggar if you can
You build on 'yes'
With your foundation most deep
Your people's roots and rear view

The Good Ol' Days

Trekked ten miles to school, five days
Barefooted, on rocks and all
Banana, cocoyam leaves, our rain covers
The good ol' days

Had one un-square meal most days
Rice we ate once a year
Santa's special delivery
The good ol' days

Salt and flour importers, I'd say
By their grace were we clothed
Our toys we built from scrap
The good ol' days

Banana bunches we transported ev'ry day
Won't trade the Memory
You who built, not break us
The good ol' days

Idea

Hate me, like me
Today, any day, I come
With two taste buds. From
two pairs of eyes, ears
I come, like a monster, spitting fire

I eat trees, rocks too
Trample on elephants and ants,
human and concrete
Trap foul air in my palms
Drain oceans dry. May replenish deserts

I bear needles of cashew belly
You may split to eat, or discard
The endangered specie, I am
Safe gate to your green age, I am
You may caress – or throw aside – in case

Of lead balls I am conceived
The pre-mature birth
That could've killed my mother
She complains still
About my overbearing weight

Issue edicts to ban me
Nay, send me to the gallows
To time I let my right or wrong
Look out for me – some day
Idea is the name, keep in mind

Northern Beach

Bikini-clad thighs
Topless hunks on these summer sands
Their pale fleshes lay, side by side
The religion of a season

Walk by, garbed
Head to toe, another breed
Foot soldiers of diktats, ways of life
A summer day on this Northern beach

Today, none pays heed – or so
To the other's being – and deeds
Mindless at daggers - daily drawn
At each other's Voice – seems the code

Like the northern goose
This hermit will fly away
To come back to these beach sands
To see how Time – great arbiter
Will settle the space question

Parent

Daddy and mommy are away
They never are home, I'd say
They're making money
A safe world for me, they say
A little pain, I fear, along the way

My little one, worry never again
With you I will remain
Today and tomorrow
A solemn bond shall we build
Forever, from this day

I'm not just a playmate
Behold, I'm your parent, any day
Will teach you all you need
To know – and not know
Have I ever failed you any way?

Knowledge is power, they say
Remember that any day
My name is TV
Some call me Idiot Box
Fools, those, I'd say

The Sextroversy

The weaker sex
Sits on the stronger sex
Controls its thoughts and actions
Source of its follies and passions
They call it the weaker sex

The weaker sex
The overblown creation
That is this generation's song
The supposed captive of a sex
They call the stronger sex

The weaker sex
Guided by those whose way of life it guides
They cocooned in a weak equation
Shortage of physical might
Equals a weaker sex

The weaker sex
Liberated for all time
Where have they hidden their eyes?
What a man can do a woman can, and..
Maybe the stronger sex?

The weaker sex?
Powerless below its master
Yet, power over its slave
The water over the fire?
T'is the equal sex

Note: *sextroversy* – the differing controversies over the
capacities of the genders

Fantasy Flight

On my wing you stood
But now I can flee – fast too
Because naked as your power over me
Was your naked sole
Unbeknown to you I pierced it
When you took a bath
With only a twig I uncovered
In this your bush of some wealth
To a safe shore this sunbird flew
When a river of blood the elephant bled

My Lords

Don't worry, said he
Brought my own mat, promised he
When out I stepped – for his water
On my mat he was sitting
I was standing

In codes spoke he
Biblical, esoteric galore,
Call me Progress, Democrazy
Freedom, Human Rights, nay
Civilization – the Way

When out of slumber I snapped
On the branch of the big apple tree he was
Digging at the roots, in the grass, I was
Weeding the Elephant's grass
His elephant feet on me, alas

Soon comes yet a visitor, I hear
Yet a name I know not
Still a mission to civilize
Guess I will just call him
My most high lord and saviour!

Downside Up

Black account
Black gold
Oiling your engines and economies
Black, as the night sky
Home of the stars that guide
Permanent with any state
Black, and shiny like ebony,
Black, as *Drew*
Warm as coal
The real *McCoy* – and them all
Black is beautiful
Ain't no whitewash
Black, *asante sana*

Notes*:*
Drew, Charles – African-American physician and medical
researcher best known for his work in the field of blood
transfusions, including the development of large-scale
blood banks in the 1940s.
McCoy, Nathaniel – African-Canadian inventor of the cup
to feed lubricating fuel to machine bearings. Issued over
50 patents in his lifetime
 asante sana – Swahili for *thank you*

Speak Now, or Forever…

I may not see mine
Still, I see your back

I will tell how crumpled that shirt
On your back is

I will be the thorn on this rose
The phlegm on the party cake

I will play god
Will you play god too?

Dream Deferred

White Prison

Socks
Gloves
Pants
Boots
Sweater
Muffler
Cap
Tie
Shirt
Jacket
Longjohn
Handkie
Liprub

Innerwear, underwear, upperwear
Thirteen to one,
Thirteen gears pin me down
Inside this my northern white prison

Note:
longjohn – worn underneath the trousers (pants) to
provide additional warmth to the legs

By Bread Alone

How can we return to the journey's path
Our umbilical cord and being,
Not the sustenance of our being,
Buried in the frozen Arctic snow?

How can we climb the moon-distance baobab
Kicking aside the ladder,
The knots of our umbilical cord,
Generations after our birth?

What punishment for the only child
Who, to help the blind granny,
Broke her only calabash –
The receptacle of the family oil

Spilled on these naked sands of time
For any to lick, the family oil?
Ephemeral, O sands of time!
As we live by bread alone

My Chief

Like you, my chief
From this village, I am
Permanently below the clouds
Of our minds
Neither houses nor inhabitants
Still, I thank you
My chief, I praise your courage
And your rule
Who said to flee when you awoke
Everyday
To meet face to face with our desert?
Chief, you must be!

The Curse

They hurled him through
Seven jungle alleys and hills
Paraded their devil through
The market square – of their borrowed minds

To the frenetic drumbeats
Of their self-appointed seers
They buried him in Devils Reserve,
On the backside of town,
Of their minds, out of sight

Curse unto your kith and kin, he cried
May you choke in your blood river
Seventy times seven times over
His plea to life denied, he wailed

Then, their devil wished them well – with a smile!

Today, these villagers of the city
Their wounds for a meal lick
Their teary fate they explain in hushed tones
Did *Osagyefo*, at the market square
Drum, gong, horn and more
Not counsel and foretell?

In the deluge of their bloody tears
Even their scorched rivers overflow

Note:
Osagyefo – ('redeemer') honorific title bestowed on
Kwame Nkrumah, Ghana's first president, whose plea
for an African political federation remains unheeded

Air Fight (The Sword, the Word)

In anger
Fingers, arms and hands
are raised

Invisible yet real
The harvest of a seed
From across seven seas
Planted, denied nurturing
Seventy times seven times over
Corked in fine metal

The harvest
The rage of youth
trapped up in the air

With arms, hands – and hoods
To a rhythm of unmasked intensity
A weapon masked
A force raw, real and potent
An enemy raw, real and potent
'T'is the Word against the Sword

Air fight
Body, Mind and Soul
The Word versus the sword

1992

Year of salvation, year of damnation
Our hats to Columbus
And his gift of a new world

After centuries of self-slaughtering
Today in one boat themselves do find
In your Victory lap minions carry your bag

Five hundred years after
and the transatlantic nightmare
The Others, waiting to exhale

Forward and together, the one marches
Backward and alone, the other staggers
Unfinished still the odes to 'sovereignty'

The serf mentality, the baggage
Of these crabs in a bowl
Dry harvests, to boot

Mimicking the *mukala*'s every sneeze and grin
Clueless, still, to grow claws, these hens
To protect the chicks from the Hawk

Cheap meat for the Hawk
Who pluck their fleshes bare
As the band rolls on for the nation

Note:
mukala – whiteman

Freedom Brand

Inside the bar of this house
We make-do on a single brand
Love it to death, our brand
Choice or none is no problem here
Honey-sweet, deceptively too
Knocks out at break-neck speed
Gives a hardened pile effect, our beer
So according to the bad mouths
We acquiesce to the verdict
Of some mad scientists and scholars
Know, they must, a clean bill of health
Does have our brand
Until then, our lovefest lives on
With Freedom
Soon, as our god we will rename
What a brand!

Cheerleaders

What you need
if not a cheerleading team
for the Olympics meet

A line of credit
We will advance, and any props, deal
To ensure our factories fill

May not do much for the stomach
Who says by bread alone lives man?
Good for morale – and this man-god

Cut the trees, plant the trees, yes sir
Cyclical, the dance of Idea
The maid of honour, revered

Of our Progress galore
As the masquerade moves on
How do we behold its beauty?

Neighbours on Freedom Street

My northern neighbour has a caterpillar
He uses once a year
My western neighbour
Plans to own one next year

My neighbour up the street has a lawn mower
His summer exercise machine
For the blades of grass of my paved lawn,
I bought mine this morning

My neighbours went camping this week
All took each the house, I think
Boat, laptop, exercise machine
Even the pepper spray, I think

So they tell me
These my eyes of metal
Fixed on my neighbours
On Freedom Street

49th Parallel Blues

From the hangman you saved my head
And cut the pump to my heart and system
With dry arteries and veins I now must choke

So how can I say my *asante*?
Your pound of flesh you expect
Any way, I suppose?

You whisked this mouse from the brute's claws
And dropped hard on a sparkling path
With broken stones, cutting deep

Quick, slow..?
How do I want
my exit?

From the desert dunes you picked this lost seed
Planted on these new England shores
And refused to water

A *Barbie* house you built me
The fields around you torched
Inside was buried my umbilical chord

The link to my past
The road to my future
How do I feel?

The pig's feces we have carried
Albeit in its intestines
The source of some nourishment is found

A shelter a body found
At whose door stands this beckoning soul?

Notes:
asante – Swahili for *thank you*
Barbie – toy; something extremely superficial and
worthless

Wooing in Hollywood!

In this back hood
The Intolerance
Of the Opium of Tolerance
Chokes the mind
As they take turns
Loving and hating
Mating and marrying,
Dating and divorcing
In a star-like twinkle
Snatching from and pushing toward the other
Hoisting, each, their trophy, ephemeral
Arrows into one another's Cupid
As they make up and break up
Love (and war) contracts and treaties
Here and there to boot

O, how variety spices
These cyclical peace-war games

Victims

Men of women, women of men
Majorities of minorities
Humans of animals

Of ideas and policies
Of partners and politricians
Of phobias and –isms

Holding us down and out
Like the long night of haunted dreams
Of a day that will not dawn

Must be our Past, our Present?
Dreaded hydra-monster of a System?
Maybe our future?

Ready our mitts
This brand New Class
To catch and pass the buck

Mu-ngang

For what you did and can do
Omnipotent and present you
That they may remember
You're but a double-edged spear
At the mercy of the hunter

We didn't summon, when we could
Omnipotent and present you
To smite and smash the witch

The fault's in we when we've used you
To smite and smash kin and kith

Stoic is the faith
Rich is the pain
For harvests, in vain

Note:
mu-ngang – medicine/magical powers; medicine-man with
some capacity to interact beyond the human world

The Captive

Caught betwixt and between
In a state of a double man
Seeks in vain the balance
Between cannons of silver-gilt savagery
and imbecile servitude
Wants independence,
To find his identity
Casts it yonder,
Accepts dependence

East of West for him?
Is home indeed, the best?
Could the monkey be right?
Is it home everywhere?
Does goodness makes its home Outside?
Does the sun rise in the north and set in the south?
Is the grass green on the other side?
Must he look north with its blinding rays?
Or south with its crippling darkness?

Aware of the cripple's dignity
Learns, still, to reject that which is his
Albeit the merits in which he sees
Even when the Shark's back's not home
Wears a double-faced mask, the captive
Is his 'bad' worse than their 'good?'
Is their 'good' better than his 'bad?'
Seeks in vain what balance
The captive

No Nobel Testament

The end of the tether I've come
Deep inside the septic tank
In esoteric wars called *acada*
I plunged as I was pushed
And told – to be made man

I fight no longer
For fraternity badges and drums
To blare the empire's hymn of thunder
Smiting kith and kin here and there
Spiteful game of fame – now lost under

Now I tread paths my own
In familiar forests and valleys
I take command on the Kilimanjaro
I paddle in steadier, surer
Deeper waters of the Congo

Soul of *Mwenumotapa*, arise
On your stones I scroll *Timbuktu*
Colonize, christianize or civilize

I can't. Won't fight in the army
of Allah, Buddha or Christ

I live for no Nobel

Notes:
acada – a perjorative reference to a highly educated
individual; education
Mwenumotapa – a highly developed civilization based on
iron technology and allied crafts that flourished in
present day Zimbabwe in the 1400s
Timbuktu – great centre of culture and learning in the
Mali and later Songhai empires

Expat (Search for an African)

Vacated and departed we have
Our fame, fortune, freedom
 In flesh and spirit to seek in our
Somalilands, our Saharas
Crumble, the house may
This foundation refuses to know

Matters not our barren pasture
Like the rest before us
Beg we will in all independence
Say, some *Mami Wata* chased us?
Nay, the fashionable thing to do

Take on each other's washing
Epasa Moto had warned, the only salvation
Followed the fairy's tale and tail
All seventy-times-seven siblings in cue.

The witch in mockery wriggles its tail

Our alien *prez* head of the cue
Three passports and accounts in hand
Chanting to a foreign ode, and still
From the left lip a half-baked patriotism
No time to retreat – the witch is all smiles

Home is where is buried our umbilical cord
Not here do we consecrate to the Call
But are served to the Maggots
For the defilement of the land
Epasa Moto we must entreat

Notes:
Expat – someone who has departed from his fatherland
to live elsewhere
Mami Wata – according to several West African legends,
underwater fairy, both revered and cursed
prez – president

Crocodile Tears

Roam like a roving ghost, I now must
In search of a fairy tale castle
Only a shadow of my glory past

Only yesterday I was pivot
On this pendulum grasshoppers danced
Snored, swayed off balance

Curses galore to you, my children
At akimbo you stood, defenseless
Mouthing a million boasts and platitudes

As the Boa smothered in its coil
The Mamba injected its venom
Into my blood veins and arteries

You rushed me to your grave, thinking mine
Intered my skeleton – your soul
In the grave of your mind, half-alive

Not even a sling did you aim at
The Hawk who keeps up the chicken swoop
Are these tears you dare to shed, now?

Dedan

Dedan, the sign
before the Boa gets me

I crawled up the Kilimanjaro to breathe it
In the air sublime around Epasa Moto
Paddled up the falling steps of the Niger
Dove into the belly of the Nile
in search of seer *Mami Wata*
Into the heart of the Equatorial
I pored in search of your trail and scent
The *mu-ngang* leaves, barks and roots too
I scraped every fissure of the Zimbabwe scrolls
In the nakedness of the *Kgalahadi*
I pulled the ears to hear it in the wind
Blowing against the shifting sands of time

Nothing

At akimbo stood your progeny
as the Boa injected its venom
into your bloodstream – our source
Rushing to inter you half-alive
We did
Trapped in the ropes
Charged to the corner by the raging Boa
The magic wand, Dedan, we need now
You took it not yonder, did you?
Spirit of the immortals, the torch
Nay, the burning spear to finish it
Before devoured by the Boa we get

Notes:

Dedan (Kimathi) – founder of the Mau Mau movement that dislodged British imperial/colonial rule out of Kenya.

Kgalahadi – (a.k.a) Kalahari

A Comedy and Murder Moment

Mouthfuls of spittle they ejaculate
Laughing over spoils of their sport
Countless *electile dysfunctions*
The carcasses of their subjects
In trenches physical and psychological
Who must choke
Unless their gods ejaculate and fart
Victims of hope in divine Providence
And smiles some life after

Note:

electile dysfunction – (coined from the medical condition, erectile dysfunction), a derogatory reference to electoral fraud and other poor governance practices.

La Vie

At sunrise we emerge
as equals
Live through the day
In steps and footprints unlike
Depart at sunset
as equals
The promise
in the day-dream of Hope
The legs for this long desert trek

Seen from Afar

The paradox of opposites
Night and day
Hot and cold
Man and woman

The one in cheek with the other
Oftentimes, belligerent

Constant, the pendulum battles for balance

Not enough
Acquire we must
Not enough room
Discard we will
As we tread the continuum
The clash between virtue and vice

Constant, the pendulum swings for balance

We will abort the children we would rather have
We will adopt the children we refused to keep
We like what we don't have
We detest what we have

Raze mountains into river valleys
Turn valleys into concrete playgrounds

In this paradox of opposites
The pendulum searches for and keeps its balance

Double Jeopardy

I complained of domination
Of home work – mine
Out to the career world I set
Better a slave to a Boss
Than at home – mine

I fled the wrath of the brute
Better a minority
Visible, audible – and damned
In a stranger's I want to call home
Than at home – mine

Father's Murderer

I am pricked by the thorns
In this their garden of roses
As I search for an iota of your nectar

Snuffed off the pungent skies
Where fly freedom's wasps
Feeding on all things and fleshes too

Where did they hide your corpse?
O, how they dance, your murderers
On the tail of this lion

Monkey See, Monkey Do

Oh how much fun they're having
The female pigs their envy could not hide
Joined the male pigs in the fray

The adrenaline rushing
Helter-skelter they all dove
Rubbed and slugged in the mud all the way

Six feet under, they are heading
To be a pig, oh what a fun time – and pride
The leveling of the longevity mudscape

Asante Cuba

Today they chant an ode
Amandla! Apartheid is dead
From the Big bush
To the Mean-and-empty streets,
The homes of broken dreams
They wrap themselves in a flag, torn
'We tricked the simpletons,' they whisper in codes
Marching to the sounds of a band, absent

A band that must play
Another tune
For another people
In another place, this time
From the Kgalahadi to the Kilimanjaro
From Aksum to Goree
Carrying the message of the drums
Of *Ogun* and *Oduduwa*
For the Cuba child far away
Lost away in their time
Ever present in the hearts
Of your sibling

Come, Cuba child, come
Sit by *Obatala*
You, the corner rock of Mwenumotapa
They tried in vain to dislodge

This band will sing and play for you
With *Ogun*, *Orisha* and *Obatala* you will dance
To the music '*Asante Cuba*'

We will sing, loud
A music running deep in our veins
Like the Nile of blood you bled in Angola
To soothe our scorched arteries
A river, thick, to blind the Shark
On which, in safety, we paddle our canoes

Dance, Cuba, dance
This morning dawns for you
The Kings of Evil
Will not drop a cowry into your bowl
Still, you will dance, Damsel Cuba
With the blood of your womb
came forth this African child
they say they celebrate

We will beat the drum
And you will dance, Cuba
Mother here understands
Never to throw the baby
with the bath water
Asante Cuba, *arriba*
For you and because of you
This morning dawns

Notes:
Arriba – (invocation) Arise
Ogun – Youruba deity of iron and other metallic Crafts
Oduduwa – Yoruba deity, progenitor of the race
Obatala – Youruba deity of Creation (of the human body)
Orisha – Yoruba deity, of the (different) Elements of
nature; the personal god

These deities form the core of the Santeria 'religion,' [a.k.a Lacumi] practiced in Cuba and which has its roots in Yoruba belief systems transported to the 'new' World by African slaves

Arriba Cuba

Arriba, Arriba, Cuba
A revolution assailed and terrorized
A revolution that dares still
To dream – and survive
Ten henchmen, fifty iron years
Too dumb and clumsy
to admit defeat
Too chicken to cross
the bridge of reconciliation
Too eager for a gory feast
Of their elephant dreams
Too oblivious to the sunbird's resolve:
Because you have learnt
to shoot without missing,
I will fly without perching
Arriba, Arriba, Cuba
Let a thousand odes ring out

Tears

Do you flow for the victim
Do you flow for the mighty
Have you been fooled
Nay, how sincere are you, and
they for whom you descend in counsel?

Do you drop on breasts
Naked, as a newborn
Or on chests putrid and heartless?
Tears, for whom do you ask us
to shed you?

Embankments do we build
against this river's surge
to cleanse the debris on the shores?

Salvation Highway

The cue was long – very long
Parents dragged unwilling offspring
For a spot on *Sci-Tech* Street

They gestured and probed, the one
Weary, they pleaded, the others
As did the Rev'rend, if only for an iota of a line

Sorry, Father, not in these times
Our religion, our salvation – nay, our damnation
We'll seek, as we stick to Sci-Tech Street

Note: *Sci-Tech* – Science and Technology

Recycled Man

Mi cann sleep!
A brother's lament rings
Profound, pervasive and persistent
Seventy times seven times over

They eyed the shirt, shoes, pants…
With a laugh, grudge and backhand
Confiscated them all
My protest in vain

'Don't you see
I wear no golden ring
That mine are hand-me-downs
That old wine now in new skin?

If you care to see deep
You will spare and grant me
the peace of sleep

Surprised, shocked and serious
They saw not my rust in their gold
As they demanded bigger, better
From their *bushfaller,* recycled

Notes:
Mi cann sleep – I can't buy sleep!
bushfaller – adventurer [one who seeks out greener pastures]

Sunken Eyes

Mi cann sleep
Tossed the brother's lament
many times over
as the Sermon of the Selfish
Who once up the fruit tree
Flushes but wild ants
down my way
As these blinkers, wide open
Shut, and then fail to sleep

Hollow Craze

Like creativity, the artist's friend
Untruthful, albeit

As time,
always faster than our pace

Angry, we become,
To overtake it

Jealous it becomes
And overtakes us

In vain we seek to move in line
With the fashion of the times

Human gods

I am busy, don't you see?
Seven seconds to save all –
Under the sun, stars and seas
The honour badge
I wear on my sleeve
For all to see
Before which all must bow

I am busy, won't you agree?
To fix the world from scratch, my call
Three hours a night
Three nights a week
Three weeks a month
Three months a year, I sleep
Lord, I am busy

My laptop, cell phone and coffee on cue
Foot soldiers of this task eternal
Can't, won't, shouldn't the latest news miss
Life-changing it might be
Can't, won't, shouldn't stop
for the Fool's game –
To smell the roses

I am busy, don't you see?
The passport to my freedom
and from your wretched life
From crib or cradle, on me ordained
Heavens, the world will miss me
Not so, vows the sunbird to the elephant
Death's embrace beckons wide, and freely

Big Apple

We can't share it
Not even in dreams
Albeit a big, fat apple

Drowned in its juice
My freedom cup flows over, and floats

You poured in tea
A magic portion, t'was

That gave birth to rabbits
And snakes

Goats
And lions

A big, sky-blue sea consumed all
Leaving me thirsty still

Inside the puree, rotten
Of this big apple

Other Side of Hell

My child eats too much
Snores
Never makes up his bed
My child is driving me mad
I weep for my child

My child is this, is that
My child is not this, not that
My child is driving me mad
I weep for my child

Her child steals
(but does not eat too much)
Smokes
(but does not snore)
Skips school
(but makes up his bed)

Walk to the other side of hell
Still weeping for my child?
Still driving me mad?

Foreign Rule

From these shores
Yesterday's transatlantic lords
May have fled
Where today's transfixed governors
Have in spirit joined them

American, English, French and in-between
The coveted passports
Harvard, Oxford, Sorbonne and whatever
Schools for the offspring
Of our absentee landlords

Still a side-lip patriotism they preach
A Trojan and barren faith
for Motherland
Of our absentee landlords
Ensconced in empireland

Pursuing hot golf courses,
Real estate – huge insurance on
the mammoth plunder
of Motherland for empireland
Vainly, they ape personhood

Stark choice, alas
when dawns the day of reckoning
for our alien citizens
when taking on slavehood
is the dark alley of no return

Black as the bank accounts
Insane, and secured in empireland

By the crazy gods of democrazy and freedom
The tears, sweat and blood
Of the victims of this our foreign rule

Democrazy Blues

I heard them talk, over and again
Promised to do this and that
Promised and promised again

For my vote, they vied
For my voice, they vowed
For the good of democracy, they vented

The ear I strained to hear
The eye I rubbed to see
me too in the deal – to no avail

Then it dawned t'was election time
When even the Wasp is a friend
Time to sting – and sing – the democrazy blues

Mosaicland

I live in Columbus Towers
Across from Old Country Street
Bordering Queen Andrew Highway
One of seventy times seven
Across the land

I attend Saint Paris University
In Sir Charles-Anne County
One of seventy times seven
Across the empire reborn
From New London to Victoryland

The name is Mary John
That, the mosaic would recognize
When, for the glory of the flag I perform
A mari usque ad mare
Any day, everyday

The fields we tilled
The rice we planted and peeled
Nothing you left me – on this table
If only in a tiny bowl and spot
Somewhere – across this land

I sweep no crumbs in my famine
From this table, and after your orgies
I bear no spot or sport
No lane after my name
Wither space or pay in the Mosaic?

Note:
A mari usque ad mar e – From sea to sea

Speaking between the Teeth

T'was good, they said
When the gander, their king, didn't take it
T'was good, they said
when the gander, our king didn't leave it

Yesterday they told papa, who believed
to fight for freedom and democracy

Today freedom's enemies raise ugly heads
left, right and centre

Today, freedom's band players and their instruments
have gone quiet

T'is bad, they say
When our king we crown
T'is good, they say
When. before this our Devil, they prostrate

Parannoyed

Pat and Sam,
my northside neighbours got married today
Pat's siblings, Chad and Sandy
came with their spouses, Chris and Jodi
As did Sam's parents, Laurie and Robin
And Pat's, Kyle and Kim
And Pat's grandparents, Terri and Kerri
As did Sam's godparents, Toni and Alex
Pastor Randy officiated

What with those different names
But a plot too many
Macho, sexist to the bone
The elephant to play king?

In the free fight of discountenance
Even the entrails of these beasts
Cannon fodder, fair and square, are

Note:
parannoyed – extremely angry

51

Cold Comfort (Pala-Pala Time)

Soft on you I will not be
'Till time renders account
Of your stewardship of this our garden

In me you will find no worldwide web
No passport to cheap glory
No 'herein lies a man for the ages'

This rose refuses to bend
Even to the gust of this wicked breeze – death songs in the air
The herald for a night-long deluge

Not even this needle's eye
Is door for the Elephant

For this Devil that excoriates the hearts
Of its own babies for a gory feast

No fraternity badges – Trojan horses
Empty titles, shall I plaster on your chest

This sacred ground you defiled
Even as you did nothing

I am cold comfort for the ugly
Name of a heartless humanity

I, Death, divorce you
Not in me shall you R.I.P.

A bed of thorny roses you sowed?

And scorn shall you reap

I see your back
This god, mad, I will play
I will aim for your balls

The Corporation

Main business line: Poverty Development
Established: 1450 or thereabout
Business factory locations: across Africa
Business headquarters: Washington
Satellite offices: London, Paris
Board of Directors: G-Seven, Paris Club
Shareholders: Civil society, Philanthropists, tourists…
Our bankers: *IMF, IBRD, CIDA, BNP*
Balance sheet: NGO (not good overall)

Notes:
Poem adapted from an original by African-Canadian poet and activist, Harold Head
IMF – International Monetary Fund
IBRD – World Bank
CIDA – Canadian International Development Agency
BNP – Banque Nationale de Paris

Egoli Blues

Spirits of the living-dead
Of a night sublime, a morning maimed
I thought I heard the echo of your call

Someone switched the skin of my birth bedhead
The scroll on which was scribbled my name
Generations before my birth

monrovia?
brazzaville?
east London?
pretoria?
anna-andrewtown?

In the name of space, what position do I play?
Forward, centre, right in or left out?
Egoli, I thought I heard the echo

Spirits of the Ancestors
Tell me, that my children I may tell
And the children of my children

Note:
Egoli – city of gold (Johannesburg, South Africa)

Boundaries

South
North
Developed
Third World
First World
Highly indebted
Left wing
Right wing…
G-Eight
Never mind one
We are the world

Our Minister

Their minister did nothing for them
Our minister past too
Still, we want our minister
Our ladder to perch our necks
Above the feculence

That tycoon, you see, is from my village
The village with no water, no road
By association are we all rich
Famous, *primus inter pares*
No, I am, you are not!

Note:
primus inter pares – first among equals

Contradiction

Foreign Aid (The Full Mouth does not Speak)

Never would they see the day
They so thought
I thought I heard them say
When god's own chosen land
Of all things beautiful, bountiful
All things foreign
The benefactor sublime
Of the wretched of the earth
Everyone and everywhere,
Would stoop to receive foreign aid

Then, the skunk's stench hit me
As raced my mind through and across
Five centuries of history
Five centuries of foreign aid
By slaves nabbed and slavery encaged,
The New World's edifices laid
Big, beautiful -and bold
By the brows, brains and breasts

And on we march to the music
Of the bold and blessed band,
This rose garden, the land
That creates, thinks, believes
And propagates miracles
Communion for the mind

Apology

Now that the work is done
What are we to do with the tools?
And what now that you have spoken
And your contrite here borne?
What can we say, nay do?
Where is our will
To drag you to the slaughterhouse
And our pound of flesh demand?

Apology
The power
Of the word over the gun

SPS (Split Personality Syndrome)

The Devil
blames the God in you

They say you are kind
I say wicked you

I see sorrow in your eyes
You feel gay, you say

On both sides of the street
Neighbours, virtue and vice, dwell

The ideal being, one in body, double in nature
Circumstance, the victor in it all

Jesus' Cargo

Five hundred plus years of haunted memory
In chains, for bondage they came
Like Judas' sacrificial lamb to the slaughter
Through the dark Middle Passage
They, in a ship called Jesus, were led
Did you hear that?
God, your name to the dogs
In a new god shall we trust?

Doublespeak – Canadiana

Assault
The state has no business in your bedroom
Child abuse
The state has no business in your bedroom
Rat assault
The state has no business in your bedroom

Gospel according to our *PET* saint
The private is not public
A slap's but self defense
unless macho its middle name
Abuse is empowerment
Unless the mane is of a macho horse

Orwellian is not our stripe
The Watch brigades and apparels
No Big Brother watching you
The public protecting over the private
The state has business in your bedroom
The private is public, no doublespeak!

Note:

PET – Pierre Elliot Trudeau [a former Canadian prime minister, the author of the declaration: *The state has no business in our bedrooms*]

The Laboratory

Our brothers and sons
Oh, what men, lucky they
From the prism of the architects
Of our blame-and-hate game

Our fathers and husbands
Gee, what pigs, poor things
Plat-de-resistance
For our blame-and-hate game

Abuser
Deserter
Molester
Predator
Did we add violent to the brew?

Brothers and sons
Fathers and husbands shall not become –
Dare not, thus doth decree
From the prism of our blame-and-hate state

Boundless is this engineer's ingenuity

Bittersweet Harvest

Yesterday she prayed
Seemed would never end, that day
For her offspring, even one, to drink, some day
from the *mukala*'s fountain

Today her mansion is the envy of the village
Today, no kid around, night or day
They've drunk all right, today
from that fountain

Who to show her, half-blind, the way
to use that techno-appliance, any day
That dream of yesterday
To take her to the village marketplace?

Life, what colour is your soul
Where did you keep your eyes
Can we have you all, ever?

Note:
mukala – whiteman

Friend or Foe (The Goat and the Grass)

You laugh with in public
Heap curses on in private
In public, talk straight with
In private, pillage the public purse with

Public demonstrations of angst
Private congratulatory bacchanals

In the daytime you complain,
Condemn, fight to defeat
At night, you covert and corrupt
Uplift, defer to

Before man, a praise hymn
Before your temples, a death plea

Between friend or foe, god or satan
I search for the spots of your shoes

On these shifting sands of time

Canine Citizen

Vintage black canine
Nine months young
Seeking serious male companion
with a non- dominant background
to share dates, birthdays
and other whisker-to-whisker moments
a hefty inheritance in the mix
Till divorce do us part

To love you
In this neck of the woods
We have only just begun
For you a government
A state we will create
And to ev'ry valley spread the good news

Father's Day Presents…

Choose from our wide selection
of today's specials
Elegant frocks and shawls
a perfect adornment
for this New Age man

Chips and cookies
Fodder for the cannon
for rounds of the name-and-blame game
Tools, and more tools
S/he still likes to think macho

And a rose, the last salvo

For this post-feminist buffoon
Beaten by the rain, its tail between its legs
S/he smiles in glee
And the experts, of their lab success

Keep those Father's Day presents coming!

Love Plantation

Welcome to our plantation
I am your co-*womyn* and host
Some thick workers we have, you can say
To admire, stake a claim
After your day's gazing
Take home – for a pump and dump
Or the cleaner's for what's left

Counsel from this plantation
The ranch cows are milked by the hour
From puberty are the cows milked
Should a work emergency call
Strap on the safety gear
Dial Senior Security Service 9-1-1

Take advantage of our offerings
the pre-dating
the pre-nuptial
the pre-sex
the pre-conception
And the post-divorce specials

The pump and dump done
We guarantee you will come back

To our love plantation
To serve you better
We are open round the clock

Note:
womyn – woman (a radical-feminist coinage)

Macho Love

This love is
 macho, domineering –
No talk-back allowed
Not how we show it, alas

The secret night meets we'll fix
Throw in the inheritance
Fight to the finish, need be
For your right to the ballot
More pet police we're hiring, or not?

Ever solemn in our pledge
(Do the shit thing, no problem)
To finish the one who will make talk
Birdie, Catie, Doggie, other fury friends,
To die to keep your no-talk-back smile

Prisms

From the south shores rays
from the north shores blind

The man who stands to pray
rubs shoulders with his god – how haughty

We are confused and enlightened
from no prism but our own

Never before have man and nature so blended
saying what we don't mean, meaning what we don't say

Like the weather, giving us
anything but our predictions

Like Creativity
Never faithful to the artist, its friend

Never before have they believed at will
not letting us know what they feel

About what we don't say and don't mean
Chameleon – from this prism

The Prism of my Prison

Stayed indoors today –
As yesterday and the day before
Now, I vow, I hate vomit

Flies, appendages bulging
Bossing all and about
Half-naked, these half-mad half-humans
Shopping carts in toe
Gadgets and cards in hand
And a certain death, this hermit will celebrate

The only smile, from a nerd
Infant soldiers of the religious army
Giant and Lilliputian pairs
Married children
Scions of the Trilogy
Progress –
Freedom –
Civilization
Or its casualties
The gods, and fodder
Of this pen's fury

Hail Epasa Moto
From behind these metal bars
My sanity I vow to keep
And survive – in this my prison

Prisoners

The colour of the street these-know not
Behind tainted glass walls they drive
Sunlight and moonlight they see not
The thickness of the earth they know not
Their walled fortresses torch heaven's gate
Air harnessed and caged they breathe
Liquid harnessed and corked they ingest
In too much dough are they steeped
Highly connected
Even from inside their concrete playgrounds
These prisoners, they complain not
The best seats in this hell these occupy

Trojan Horse

Mendacity run amok
Picking its casualties,
The minions of a mind,
By the millions
Like the dry season locusts
Across our savannahs
The left hand playing slave to the right
The right foot asking the left for direction

The Trojan horse
Like a breeze, only, from the desert
Lurking a harmattan
Ready to raze barren – with notice or none

To plunder, not extol
The source of this infested swamp

The deference –
Of the bee that gives honey
And stings too

Place

What's this allegiance, near religious
To find you, our umbilical cord ?
We have, we must, come back
Seems the verdict from Epasa Moto
The rock we must push
Up to our grace – and grave

On you, this garden
No corn we planted
Still, we must return
When tend you, we can't

Identity Crisis

I curse, I hail
This Satan of God
You demon or deity in control
Two heads of a coin, nay, birds of a feather?
I seek to find the master or the servant – in whom?

The great reductionist
From your throne –
Giving and taking all life
Object of my hate, can't have you
Hope of my dreams, love you to death

Do you come through putrid paths
paved with gold but bearing thorns?
Are you this bundle of joy,
Comfort on the breasts
of this woman, once barren?

Money, who, what indeed are you?

The Trail

The sweat of fathers and mothers
Past and present
Lodged in overseas havens
By any means thinkable
It would scream, if it could talk
Being made a roller-coaster
Like the clamour of they
Who expect *their* money
Back,
Any day, anyhow, after all
By any Western means

The Fisherman's Drag-net

This fisherman's drag-net
Traps shrimps
And sharks too

These come fleeing
from even the shadows of their devils
Those, from the shadows of their inner devils
the just rewards of their satanic past
To breathe, seek peace and freedom
To enjoy their booty
They all flock and squeeze through
This drag-net with plenty of crevices

Here, peace, freedom do not discriminate
Have not taste, colour, size
Are not selfish, peace and freedom
We must all have
Victims and criminals

Fisherman, where is the headlight
To see your drag-net's haul?

Honourable-Chief-Doctor-Alhaji-Architect X

Like hot air balloons, their titles loom large
Across every space, physical and human
Alien sophistry, they choke the mind and mouth

Humongous, these balloons
Full of foul air, they're picked and defecated
At life's many playstations and crucifixes

Lofty legacies, absent still
But the trampling of a million pairs of elephant eyes
From bands of prostrating sycophants

The big glory for these human flies, and serfs
To feast on their moving carcasses
Their rocks of Sisyphus they dare to reify

Wallowing, they must, under the weight
Of cacophonic mysterious mumblings
Harbingers of maleficent maelstroms

Honourable-Chief-Doctor-Alhaji-Architect X

The mindscape and landscape must stay barren
Defiled, through sins of commission and omission
And the bandit band blares on

To Epasa Moto the longest entreaty yet
To wrestle these riff-raffs from our basket brains
Before sink our canoes in these rivers of our blood

Honourable-Chief-Doctor-Alhaji-Architect X…
Hah!

Sand, Sea, Sun and Sex

For this quartet, this *sextination*
From around the globe
They flock, take on you,
Beautiful Mama J and friends
Day and night, all year round

A prostitute is a substitute
For our enemy-lovers
Souls sold to the gods of I-Me-Mine
Assassins of the angel of love
Buried in the backyard

All year round, they may dump on you
Not today, Mama J, and sisters
The steady rock on the shore, you remain
Thank you beautiful Mama J, and siblings
No problem, any time

Note:
sextination – a place frequented for sexual gratifications

Black and White in Love and Hate

As yesterday and tomorrow
Today they quarrel on matters even benign
As the hate of each other's being

In between, these enemy-lovers
As yesterday and tomorrow, will die
For a moment in the other's head and skin

Dying for the tan and locks, here
Creaming the skin, stretching the hair, there
Back and forth, dying for the other's stead
Still, the other they hate
To admit they love inside to belong
If only for a flirtatious moment spared

On Savages and Civilization

Look at that, look at them, I say
Screaming circuses
Fists and feet raised to the face
Defer to, they seem to must
Some sport gods
Here, there are no savages

Had you sown the poisoned seed
Of this weird wild weed
Gun-ordained proof it would be
Of your savagery

Nay, look at you, tamed
Who bore no boxing
Fathered no football
Hatched no hockey
Raised no rugby game
Uncivilized, you are all the same

I refute yet a poetic sermon
Your charge, until proven innocent, of guilt
Your pretensions to perfection
Sold by a million smooth-tongued high priests
Oh, what 'magnificent specimens of your savage
manhood'
Alas, here there are no savages!

Searching for Satan

See them, hear them, fat chance
Across the land their stench, alas
We see, hear and feel
And speak to, still

A marauding Plague
bribing
corrupting
prostituting
body and soul
For bidders high and low

Blame and complain, our solo chant
Parading our victimhood across the land
Like a noble badge
before a morbid Plague
begging
crying
praying
for a better day
Playing the saint, still

Blind, as Night's shadow
That Satan within each
Won't come out of the hood, still

Not on this street
Satan lives not here

Nationality: Villageois

Think big?
Never heard it, I swear
Inside this box I vow to remain

Minds small
Like our national village
Only to perish, we think flourish

In smallness
Chasing the fleeing rat
Abandoning the burning house, they do

The city, you dread
The bright lights, big
Will blind, not illuminate the path

My cup
Is half empty, never half full
Villageois is my nationality

Caged in
Somalias, our comfort zones
This victimhood, our place ordained

Nationality, foreigner
Ah, vector of violent crime
If I'm bad, the fault's in them

Villageois, my nationality
On my sleeve shall I carry
Forever

Note:
Villageois – backward

Can't Cure Cancer

Because I am developed
And you are not
I will serve you soup
After I lick the ladle I will use

What foreign aid did you give me?
Over the centuries, you say?
Still, I am developed
And you are not

Batter and punch ourselves to a pulp
In circuses we baptized sports
Still, we are developed
And you are not

Divorce, rape, prostitution
Pornography, sex tourism – what problems?
My Freedom, my Rights insignias
I am developed, you are not

The swing and homosexuality, too
Proof of my Tolerance – Weakness, not
Ask Freedom's other casualties?
Yet, I am developed, you are not

Every nook and cranny near and far
This Great Good renamed after
Every nook and cranny of motherland

New York, New England, Franceville

This, my Racism and Intolerance
Towards the other, you dare say?
Because fountains of Patriarchy
And barbaric too, they are

'Cause for my Mrs Vatican and the bible
This god is a Celt, not some tribe
I am developed, you are not

Can't cure cancer, can make disease
For his slaughterfests he summons
The precision of the *WMD*, not machete
See, he is civilized, you are not

Note:
WMD – weapon of mass destruction